Acknowledgements

I would like to thank Jane Ashworth, Jane Barrett, Leonora Lloyd and Mike Marqusee for their assistance in reading and commenting on this manuscript. Any errors, of course, are my responsibility.

LIZ DAVIES

GW00706012

Feminism after Post-feminism

Liz Davies

Liz Davies is a barrister and Labour Councillor in Islington. She is Chair of Islington Council's Women's Committee. This pamphlet is written in her personal capacity.

From the beginning, feminism has challenged the existing structure of society. It is hardly surprising, then, that feminism and feminists have always found themselves under attack. In the 1970s, during the rise of the 'Second Wave' of feminism, the activists of the Women's Liberation Movement, derided as 'women's libbers', found themselves caricatured as bra-burning man-hating women with chips on their shoulders, ugly and unable to attract members of the opposite sex, obsessed with apparent trivia such as changing language. I was twelve years old when the Sex Discrimination Act came into force in December 1975, and I vividly remember television newscasters, men and women, joking that from now on Manchester would have to be called 'Personchester'.

Despite the campaign to trivialise the women's movement, feminism fought its way into the popular consciousness, and secured structural and legislative changes. The late 1960s and 1970s saw the Abortion Act, divorce law reform, the Equal Pay Act and Sex Discrimination Act, increasing numbers of women in higher education and in the professions, maternity rights, women's refuges, and increased reporting of rape and domestic violence. A number of attempts to water down the Abortion Act were fought off by feminists and, in 1979, by an alliance of feminists and the TUC against the Corrie Bill.

On the left, there were elements deeply critical of feminism. Feminists were portrayed as man-haters in many male-dominated left groups. It was argued that the root of women's oppression was an economic one and that feminists concentrated too much on the slogan 'the personal is political'. It was said that feminists ignored the concept of class, that many of the social gains that feminists advocated (child-care, reproductive rights, the right to personal safety) could only be achieved after a working-class revolution. Many male left activists resisted examining their own behaviour and found themselves in difficulties when 'the personal is political' was used to challenge male sexual practices within left organisations.

But feminism made a deep impact on the left. The argument that socialism necessarily included the liberation of women, and that women's liberation required more than mere economic change, became widely accepted. Feminists on the left argued for greater representation of women and for the right of women to organise autonomously, for the use of language which did not exclude women, and for changes in men's behaviour towards women. It was increasingly recognised that when women mobilised for economic and social change they necessarily challenged many of the institutions which bolstered the status quo. It was therefore not only women who benefited from this movement but all those who suffered under the present system. Many left groups had their own women's sections or publications, which were overtly feminist as well as socialist. The picture was not entirely rosy, as was made clear in *Beyond the Fragments*,[1] the classic depiction of the difficulties of being a feminist and a socialist, and fitting into no clear grouping. However, by the end of the 1970s, many of the ideals of feminism had become incorporated into the ideology of the left, and were making inroads into public life as a whole.

Today there is a new attack on feminism. Susan Faludi has characterised it as the 'backlash' against feminism.[2] Feminists are now constantly informed that feminism is out-of-date, that our goals have been achieved and are therefore no longer relevant, or even that these goals were socially destructive and that the changes wrought by feminists need to be reversed. As right-wing ideologues re-assert the pre-eminence of the family as a unit of social organisation, feminists are held responsible for a supposed breakdown of family values. The 'man-hating' myth endures. It is claimed that men have suffered under feminism, and that their demands and needs must now be catered to. Most perniciously, feminism has been painted as doing women no favours, as having created a generation of working women whose lives are more difficult and less rewarding than their mothers and grand-mothers. The new anti-feminists attack the women's movement for being factional, pre-occupied with the plight of lesbians or black women or other groups, and increasingly out of touch with the experience of 'ordinary women' (and never mind that many of 'ordinary women' are lesbians or black or both).

The demonising of feminists continues, not only in the tabloid press but in broadcast journalism and academia. Two years ago, when I appeared as a panellist on a radio discussion on the relevance of feminism, a male questioner in the student audience said that though the feminists on the panel seemed perfectly nice people he would be scared of speaking to us at a party if he knew we were feminists.

These attacks take place in the context of a worldwide ideological debate informed by post-modernism. We are told that we have reached 'the end of history', that there is no such thing as progress and that the era of 'grand narratives' of rational social transformation is over. The ideal of equality is downgraded, as is collective political activity. Ironically, post-modernism's 'de-centering' relativism derives in part from the feminist critiques of language, literature and history. Equally, the post-modern emphasis on the politics of personal identity finds some of its roots in the feminist slogan 'the personal is political'. But in 'identity politics', distinctions and decisions are made on the basis of personal identity rather than political programme. When I was active in the student movement in the mid-80s, we labelled the identikit female student politicians whose sole election manifesto would be 'vote for me, I'm a woman', as 'femocrats'[3] — identity politics without the politics. Thus what was originally an attempt to analyse politically every aspect of women's lives, an assertion that no activity was free from politics, has been used to sidestep political arguments. Just as post-modernism depoliticises political activity, so post-feminism depoliticises feminism.

All these phenomena are reflected in the labour movement in Britain. Feminism challenged the programme and structures of the labour movement, and some of its ideas have been incorporated into mainstream labour movement policy and practice. But in recent years, while identity politics have boosted the careers of a handful of women politicians, women's demands have taken a back seat and real power for grass-roots women has been curtailed. As the British labour movement becomes increasingly depoliticised, so does women's activity within the movement. Influential think-tanks such as the Institute for Public Policy Research and Demos are now calling for a reappraisal of fundamental feminist assumptions and demands. And the Labour Party's policy on women has become more and more a question of image, with ever fewer substantial commitments.

In this pamphlet I set out to examine and answer the 1990s attacks on feminism, and to reclaim feminism from the post-feminists. I started reading and thinking about feminism in the late 1970s, and have been active in feminist campaigns and labour movement politics ever since. To me, feminism and socialism are indivisible. My experience tells me that feminism has had a number of important achievements, and that we still have a long way to go.

Has feminism succeeded?

Feminism, it is said, has achieved many of its original goals and young women today no longer need to be feminists. This argument suggests that, at some unspecified date following the birth of second-wave feminism, there was a Golden Age when our demands for equality were recognised and fulfilled. I must have blinked and missed it.

The seven demands of the Women's Liberation Movement, drawn up at founding conferences in the early 1970s, were:
- free 24 hour child-care;
- equal pay now;
- abolition of the legal definition of women as dependent on men;
- equal education and job opportunities;
- an end to discrimination against lesbians;
- free abortion and contraception on demand;
- freedom for all women from intimidation by the threat or use of violence or sexual coercion, regardless of marital status; an end to all rules, assumptions and institutions which perpetuate male dominance and men's aggression towards women.

In Britain, how many of these demands have been achieved, and to what extent?

The legal definition of women as dependent on men has been largely abolished. Women can now formally access welfare benefits, bank loans and tax concessions in their own names. It is common for couples to own property jointly. Many women retain their own surnames after marriage.

Certainly, access to higher education and to the professions for women has improved. Over 50% of law and medicine graduates are now women.[4] Women can be architects, journalists, editors of national newspapers, politicians, soldiers, brick-layers and even Prime Minister! But this increase in access has primarily benefited middle-class women.

Child-care is increasingly regarded as essential, rather than a luxury. Employers are introducing work-place nurseries and 'family-friendly' policies in attempts to retain women employees. Child-care is now a major political demand: the Tories offer nursery vouchers, while Labour local authorities attempt to fund public-sector child-care centres.

With developments in medicine, women have achieved far more control over their reproductive rights. Abortion may not be available on demand, but it is available on the NHS and relatively accessible to women. Contraception is widely used and young girls are getting better, and more, sex education.

Despite cuts in higher education, women's studies courses and feminist discourse have flourished in the academic world.

The Equal Pay Act has been broadened in scope to encompass the European Community concept of equal pay for work of equal value. The concept of sex discrimination at work has been broadened to include sexual harassment at work and rights for part-time workers. Both public-sector and private-sector employers have responded to demands for changes in working conditions: flexible working-hours, paternity or parental leave, maternity provision designed to retain the loyalty of women employees.

Women are better represented at a political level. Women's parties have stood in a number of elections in different countries, including recently in the Northern Irish election where their votes brought them 2 seats at the peace talks. Women are active in all main political parties as Councillors and office-holders. Yet women's representation in Parliament has hardly improved at all: 9% of the members of the House of Commons today are women, in comparison to 4.6% in 1964.

Rape and domestic violence are now prosecuted as serious crimes. After a 1982 Thames TV documentary exposed the cavalier way in which a rape victim was treated by the police, the police began to set up specialist rape suites, and ensured that women police officers dealt with rape victims. The reporting of rape has increased as women have greater confidence that their reports will be taken seriously, and that they will be dealt with sympathetically. Rape in marriage is now a crime and victims of rape are not supposed to be asked about their sexual history in Court.

Domestic violence, which can affect the lives of one woman in three[5] and is therefore a real prospect in the life of every woman, is now investigated far more seriously by the police, who have established a number of specialist Domestic Violence Units and are no longer supposed to record calls as 'just a domestic incident'. Domestic violence refuges have found their funding substantially cut by local authorities, but many still survive. More and more women seek injunctions to protect themselves from violent partners. Domestic violence is recognised in the government Code of Guidance on Homelessness as a legitimate reason why a woman would be homeless.

Whilst lesbians can still formally be discriminated against as lesbians (the Sex Discrimination Act does not prohibit discrimination on the grounds of sexuality), there are an increasing number of challenges to discrimination against lesbians in the Courts. The Labour Party is committed to legislating to end discrimination on the grounds of sexuality. Lesbians have become more visible, in the entertainment industry and generally in public life. For the first time, the Labour Party has an out lesbian standing as a Prospective Parliamentary Candidate. The rise of 'chic' lesbianism certainly has its critics: the media obsession with Madonna, k.d. Laing and others leaves one with an uncomfortable sense that heterosexual male fantasies are being gratified. But visibility is a step forward.

There have been gains and these gains are the result of the activities of a multifaceted women's movement. But is there true equality between men and women? Can we all go home and stop fighting?

The reality

Despite the Equal Pay Act and Sex Discrimination Act, women still only earn 79% of men's earnings.[6] Whilst women have formally broken through into many of the professions, the glass ceiling operates to prevent them rising in those professions in the same numbers as men. Only 9.8% of managers are women.[7] Women in law and medicine, who graduate in equal numbers to men, find that once they qualify advance to the higher echelons is often blocked. In the solicitor's profession twice as many men as women achieve partnership; more women than men drop out from the Bar; in medicine, only 38% of senior house officers are women, and only 24% of registrars.[8]

Within areas of employment more traditionally filled by women, there is still a disproportionately high number of male managers. In the teaching profession, for example, men and women work in roughly equal proportions, but 78% of headteachers in secondary schools are male.[9] In primary schools, men constitute 19% of the teaching workforce overall, but 50% of headteachers in England and Wales. The glass ceiling may operate against women in traditionally male areas of employment, but men in traditionally female areas continue to find it relatively easy to achieve promotion.

Women are more active economically, but they are still on average paid less than men and there has been little breakdown in traditional gender distinctions in employment. Whilst 65% of women now participate in economic activity (wage-earning) — compared with 53% in 1973[10] — many of those women are concentrated in part-time and/or low-status jobs. Time out for child-birth and child-rearing can cost an average woman £202,500 in wages foregone.[11] Four out of five women are still working in service industries: catering, cleaning, hairdressing, etc.[12] In 1990 only 7% of women manual workers earned over the male manual average, and one-third of all women earned less than half of the male average.[13] Whilst there has been an increase in child-care places, allowing women more flexibility to go out to work, the supply comes nowhere near filling the demand. And the burden of domestic work has hardly shifted: among couples where both partners work, in 67% of cases women do *all* the domestic work. On average, women do an extra fifteen hours unpaid (domestic) work per week more than men.

Women are still poorer overall than men. The poverty rate for female-headed households is 150% more than the national average. Female-headed households are also more likely to live in rented accommodation than own their own home.

Whilst domestic violence is now treated as a crime, the fact that one in three women will experience it at some time of their lives is a frightening indictment of a society which has utterly failed to achieve inter-personal equality and respect. Feminists have been campaigning against domestic violence for over twenty years, yet there is no evidence that incidents of domestic violence have lessened at all. Remedies may be available for women fleeing domestic violence, but they are limited. Court injunctions can be ineffective and (as fewer of the population are eligible for legal aid) prohibitively expensive. The provision of refuge space is declining as local authorities cut their budgets. Campaigns such as the Edinburgh and London Zero Tolerance campaigns, run by Labour local authorities, were welcomed as an attempt to change male attitudes to domestic violence. But the domestic violence statistics suggest that attitudes will take a long time to change, and many women will be injured (and some die) before domestic violence is eradicated.

There have been improvements in the prosecutions of rape, but at the same time the media is increasingly pre-occupied with distinguishing the 'deserving' from the 'undeserving' among rape victims. A series of date-rape cases have resulted in highly-publicised acquittals. The only serious rape is portrayed as rape by a stranger, despite statistics that show that the overwhelming majority of women who are raped are raped by a man known to them.[14] Rape and other sexual assaults are the least successful prosecutions undertaken by the police and the Crown Prosecution Service. At each stage in the prosecution process, complaints of sexual assault are less likely to succeed than complaints about other forms of assault — from the initial reporting stage (where 38% of all complaints are 'no crimed', i.e. not proceeded with) through plea bargaining and the downgrading of offences to the final trial.[15]

The real impact of feminism seems to have been in changing women's expectations. Recent studies have made much of surveys revealing that young women do not describe themselves as 'feminists' or identify with feminists. However, the same surveys also show that women expect not to have to choose between work and family, that they expect equal pay and equal treatment at work, and that they expect to be able to live their lives without fear of assault, whether from a stranger or at home. In 1995, the Women's Communications Centre carried out a survey of over 10,000 women, through postcards distributed through the Body Shop. The result showed that women's demands reflected those of the feminist movement: equality at work, not to be judged by appearances, the equal sharing of domestic tasks with men, together with wider demands for an end to war, better health and education, a concern for the environment and action against poverty.[16] Unfortunately the price of this publication, £125 for companies, £46 for non-profit making organisations, placed it well out of the reach of ordinary feminists or women's groups.

In the last quarter of a century, feminism has developed and matured. There are certainly sharp debates within feminism, but these are part of the process of developing ideas and learning from each other that must take place in any political movement. Most difficult is probably the pornography debate, which has found some feminists uneasily aligned with right-wing and religious activists, whilst others gingerly try to identify distinctions between pornography and eroticism (distinctions that will always be difficult when the material is largely aimed at male heterosexual consumers). Black women and lesbians have rightly argued for their voices to have the same legitimacy as those of white, heterosexual women. All political movements argue out different and new analyses. Sometimes that process can be destructive, and at other times highly creative. The labour movement has wrestled with racism, sexism and heterosexism, but few would claim that it is fundamentally split by these debates, which is what is often alleged in regard to the women's movement. In practice, feminists tend to learn from their sisters and an increased diversity within the movement is a strength, not a weakness.

Who has lost out through feminism?

The most pernicious aspect of the backlash is the claim that feminism has in fact done women no favours. Susan Faludi cites as an example the Glenn Close character in the film *Fatal Attraction*, a woman who seems to have foregone a family in order to build her career and finds herself, towards the end of her child-bearing years, without a man or a child. A brief affair with Michael Douglas turns her into a homicidal maniac, attempting to destroy Douglas's happy family (in which traditional mother-father roles are respected) in order to win his love and have his children. The underlying thesis is that feminism turns you into a barren, homicidal maniac! This attack is not just confined to film-imagery. Faludi cites the Harvard-Yale study, which received national headlines in the United States when it predicted a 'marriage crunch' among baby-boomer women graduates. Its methods were later scientifically discredited.

The backlash can also be found in writings by women aimed explicitly at women, from inside and outside the feminist movement. Both Camille Paglia and Naomi Wolf, although writing from ostensibly different standpoints, blame feminism for something they define as 'victim-feminism'.

In *The Beauty Myth*[17] Wolf, deploying a feminist analysis, debunked the emphasis on women's appearance and detailed how this emphasis affects women in practice — eating disorders, the treatment of appearance as an occupational qualification, the huge fashion and cosmetics industry. This was not a new thesis — Susie Orbach had expounded it in *Fat is a Feminist Issue* in 1978.

Wolf's achievement was the detailed research she mustered in support of the case. But since Wolf believes that one of the most unpopular aspects of feminism has been its identification with a readiness to blame men for all social ills, she is so anxious to avoid being criticised for the same thing that she refuses to acknowledge that men, as individuals and collectively, can and do benefit from the beauty industry. The only prescription she offers for overcoming the 'beauty myth' is for individual women to change. 'The toughest but most necessary change will come not from men or from the media, but from women, in the way in which they see and behave towards other women.'

In *Fire with Fire*,[18] Wolf goes further, attacking what she calls 'old feminism' and arguing that women will become powerful through their individual characteristics, a concept she describes as 'power feminism'. In an extraordinary narrative, designed to argue the importance of making money, she describes receiving relatively substantial royalties from the publication of *The Beauty Myth* and the process that she went through, from guilt at the amount of money she was earning to welcoming substantial earnings as liberating. She argues that feminism has created a new consciousness at the very top of political society, citing President Clinton as 'pro-feminist'. Three obstacles stand in the way of further advance: 'many women have become estranged from their own movement; one strand of feminism has developed maladaptive attitudes; and women's lack of psychology of female power to match their new opportunities'. Her concern, once she has attacked the feminist movement, is to concentrate on women improving themselves: 'how we can retrieve that wild child — the inner bad girl — in order to embrace those qualities of leadership and sexual self-possession, and the solid sense of entitlement that we are conditioned to disavow in ourselves, and to resent in other women.' Her prescription fits in neatly with the current fashion for self-help psychology books. It is effectively an argument for the status quo — women need to change themselves, not society, and an argument for women to become more like men.

Wolf recently caused controversy by using her own experience of pregnancy to argue that the feminist call for abortion on demand was misguided. Wolf may be perfectly well-intentioned, and she has every right to enjoy her pregnancy, but it was revealing that she seemed unaware that the feminist demand has never been that women are *required* to have abortions, simply that each woman should have the right to choose whether she will have a child or not, unconstrained by the views of priests, legislators or opinion formers. Wolf's distortion of the feminist demand, in order to attack it, only plays into the hands of anti-abortion campaigners.

Camille Paglia[19] seems anxious to blame feminists for most of the evils of the world. Her concept of 'victim-feminism' is a direct attack on feminist self-help. She regards domestic violence as something that women can prevent if they choose: 'any woman who stays with her abuser beyond the first incident is complicitous with him'. She goes further than that and argues that the woman is responsible for domestic violence even before the first assault on her:

'What leads up to the first blow is always the same: provoked or not, she has pushed his buttons of dependency. Once again, he faces his insignificance in women's eyes. He has dwindled back to boyhood, where women ruled him. To recover his adult masculinity, he lashes out at her with his fists. He savours her pain and fear, but her refusal to defend herself takes the fight out of him. He is sickened, desperate, apologetic.'[20]

The message from Paglia is that it is women's responsibility, not men's, to avoid domestic violence. Research shows that, on average, abused women will have been subject to violence some 37 times before they manage to leave their abuser.[21] There are many practical problems preventing women leaving — the prospect of homelessness, financial dependence on their husband/boyfriend, children — as well as cultural pressure and the hope that their abuser will change (as he will usually promise to). In an ideal society, where obtaining support, rehousing, children's schools, etc. was easy, and where women were financially independent, maybe women who stayed with their abuser would be 'complicitious', but to argue as Paglia does in this society betrays a profound ignorance of the reality of women's lives. In fact, Paglia's attack on what she calls 'victim-feminism' amounts in the end to a head-in-the-sand denial that sexual harassment exists, that rape by a man known to the woman exists, or that there are any barriers to women's progress other than their own reluctance.

Paglia refuses to believe that any sexual harassment exists, and reserves her worst vitriol for Anita Hill (whom she calls 'wily') and her supporters. The women she admires are right-wing, privileged, women such as Margaret Thatcher. Indeed, she proposes Thatcher as a role-model for any aspiring woman politician. 'If we are ever to have a woman President, she must, like Thatcher, demonstrate her readiness to command the military.'[22]

Clearly, the notion that women are responsible for the inequality in their lives is ridiculous, whether coming from a supposedly feminist standpoint such as Wolf's, or an explicitly anti-feminist standpoint such as Paglia (Paglia defines herself as a feminist, but attacks all the existing feminist organisations). Both women have become 'celebrity' feminists and have far more access to the media than any feminist seeking to defend the movement. And both women see liberation entirely in individual terms, disregarding history, which shows that gains have come about not through the likes of Margaret Thatcher, but through the collective action of women.

The backlash also encompasses a claim that men have lost out, and that it is time now to concentrate on men's needs. This claim manages both to attack feminism directly and to insinuate itself into feminism. Robert Bly and his Iron Johns believe men are becoming 'soft', and that modern man needs to get back in touch with his 'wild side'.[23] There is a whole literature of 'me-tooism'

— characterised in Britain by Neil Lyndon who argues that the feminist agenda has resulted in men working longer hours, being excluded from family life and (most amazingly) that men are more at risk of domestic violence from women than women are from men. Writing in *The Guardian* he quotes a survey that 11% of men have been violently attacked by the women they live with and that 6% of women have been violently attacked by the man they live with. 'Why does the feminist-led Left go on repeating the lie that women are in physical danger of attack from men?' he asks. It is an inversion of reality so extreme that it defies rational analysis.

More sophisticated and serious arguments have been made to the effect that in order to change society we must change social attitudes, particularly among men. This has always been one of the goals of the women's movement, but here too, the centre of attention has shifted. It is no longer men who must listen to women and change accordingly, but women who must listen to men (as if they do not do a great deal of this already) and become sensitive to their needs. The Equal Opportunities Commission reports that men are now approaching them for assistance with sex discrimination claims in equal numbers to women. This could be interpreted as a sign that men, rather than women, are now discriminated against as a group. An alternative explanation is that men are rather quicker than women to perceive grievances, and may well perceive the appointment of a woman rather than a man as due to positive discrimination rather than the woman's ability.

The most overtly political attack on feminism emanates from the right-wing 'family values' agenda. The attack on single mothers has come from, among others, Peter Lilley, Secretary of State for Social Security, who claims that single mothers become pregnant in order to obtain Council housing, and Tony Blair, who went out of his way to proclaim that children are better off brought up by two (heterosexual) parents than by any other family forms. A picture is painted by Tory tabloids such as the *Daily Mail* in which children brought up by single parents are held responsible for most of society's ills. In fact, despite the increase in divorce, statistics show that children are still overwhelmingly brought up by both natural parents. In 1979, 84% of children were living with both natural parents, falling only to 80% in 1985. Most of those living with one parent have frequent contact with the other. And very few single parents started out as single parents — most children were born to a heterosexual relationship which later broke up. Despite the reality, feminism is portrayed as an influence causing the break-up of the family and hence every sort of social ill conceivable.

Families Need Fathers combines the resurrection of family values with male 'me-tooism'. They argue that a child's right to know and have contact with his/her father should take precedence over considerations of the mother's and child's safety. They have been most effective in mobilising public opinion against the Child Support Act. Feminist critiques of the Child Support Agency (including objections to the pressure it puts on women to remain in contact with violent men, and the Agency's failure to alleviate child poverty in any way) were lost in the barrage of complaints from men and their second wives.

Most recently, family values surfaced in the *Daily Mail*'s campaign against the Domestic Violence and Family Homes Bill and the Family Law Reform Bill. The Domestic Violence and Family Homes Bill was an innocuous piece of legislation, designed to consolidate the existing civil law remedies for women fleeing domestic violence. Shortly before the end of its passage through Parliament, the *Daily Mail* ran a campaign denouncing it as a feminist charter, which would allow women to require men to leave their homes, whether or not the couple were married. In fact, that provision has been law since 1976 — in the Domestic Violence and Matrimonial Proceedings Act. The Tory right responded to the *Daily Mail*'s call and within days the Bill was withdrawn by the government. The Family Law Reform Bill restricts access to divorce, by requiring couples to seek compulsory mediation before starting the divorce proceedings. Despite this, its provisions were not severe enough for the now rampant Right, which wanted to add yet further restrictions.

Whilst domestic violence is generally taken more seriously than it was in the early days of the feminist movement, male violence against children is still widely downplayed. After the mid-80s child abuse scandals, a body of psychological opinion developed the concept of 'false memory syndrome'. Whilst there certainly must be safeguards for the accused when children disclose that they have been abused or adults disclose that they were abused as children, the obsession with 'false memory syndrome' shifts any criminal interrogation away from the alleged abuser to the child or adult disclosing the abuse. Like rape victims, children subject to child abuse are made to feel that they are the ones on trial. Despite the many high-profile child abuse scandals, there is a refusal to acknowledge that overwhelmingly it is heterosexual men who abuse children. Where women are involved, usually they are complicit in their silence rather than direct participants in abuse. Instead of analysing child abuse as analogous to the problem of male violence against women, the media paints it as a rarity involving sick minds, male or female, and largely perpetrated by gay men against little boys.[24]

No longer a feminist movement?

The final attack on feminism takes the form of a lament. Some feminists active in the 1970s are given platforms to regret the supposed lack of feminist activity in the 1990s. We are told that women no longer call themselves feminists. In fact, the statistics are contradictory. A *Cosmopolitan* survey[25] found that only 38% of young women described themselves as feminist, although 75% described themselves as ambitious. Given the bad press feminism has constantly suffered over the years, I think 38% is quite high and probably unchanged since the 1970s. Another survey in the

United States found that 51% of women identified themselves as feminists[26] — and that the figure rose to 71% when the women were provided with a dictionary definition of feminism. That is surely the point: what matters is not whether women describe themselves as feminist, but whether they subscribe to the goals of feminism, above all the goal of equality, and all surveys suggest that they do.

Whether there really has been a decrease in feminist activity since the 1970s is more difficult to determine. Probably the 'Reclaim the Night' marches were the most overt and popular feminist political activities in the 1970s, involving the largest number of women. Activities such as protests at beauty contests were more flamboyant and therefore attracted more press interest than the numbers of participants warranted.

Certainly there is no longer an equivalent of 'Reclaim the Night' marches. Campaigns dealing with women's safety and security have become mainstream, such as the local authority funded Zero Tolerance campaign. Many practical feminists have concentrated on the nitty-gritty of safety, working for Rape Crisis or domestic violence refuges. But political activity organised by and for women has continued: from popular campaigns waged by women at Greenham Common and Women Against Pit Closures, active both in 1984-5 and again in 1992 (when a number of women occupied pits to prevent closures) to industrial actions comprising mainly women workers — from Grunwicks in 1978, through the nurses' actions in the late 80s, the Burnsalls' and Pall Mall Hillingdon Hospital strikers in 1996. Feminists still come together to fight off attacks on abortion — as in the Fight the Alton Bill campaign in 1988. And in America, in recent years, the pro-choice lobby has mobilised demonstrations of half a million and more. Across the world, as women come into contact with the globalised economy and multi-national corporations, they have taken the lead in thousands of environmental, economic and human rights campaigns, such as the Chipko Andolan in Uttar Pradesh, where women villagers organised to embrace trees to block the destruction of their environment by commercial forestry.

Whilst there are no longer feminist conferences as such, there are a large number of women's conferences within the labour movement which have feminist agendas and conferences on specific women's issues such as safety, domestic violence or equality in employment. The demise of *Spare Rib* was certainly a blow, as will be that of *Everywoman* if it folds, but other feminist publications soldier on and new ones will always emerge.

The loss of many local authority Women's Committees and Women's Units has also been hailed as an indication of the end of feminism. I write as Chair of a local authority Women's Committee, and someone who has consistently fought to retain a separate Women's Committee in the face of large-scale local authority spending cuts. Certainly, the loss of many Women's Committees has had an impact on local government. During the mid-1980s, when many Labour local authorities set up Women's Committees, local government services were under constant scrutiny, both by paid officers with an equal opportunities brief and by local women, to ensure that services were responsive to women's needs, and accessible to local women. Women's Committees funded a number of women's groups, usually working on safety, self-defence or health, and staged large-scale consultations with local women. At their best, they were accountable to local women and were part of a broader movement to improve public services for women. Now that many Women's Committees have been abolished, local government services are no longer under the same detailed scrutiny and there is no longer the same link and consultation with local women.

But there were always difficulties with Women's Committees, especially their role in funding women's groups. Undoubtedly, the funding for women's groups was a major advance for the feminist movement, and freed many feminist campaigners from the arduous process of constantly raising money to make ends meet, and allowed them to pay campaign workers a decent wage. The downside was that many groups became completely dependent on local government funding. Many collapsed when their local Women's Committee was abolished and the funding withdrawn. Activists in the National Abortion Campaign, which is still a vibrant, campaigning organisation, attribute its longevity to the fact that it was never dependent on local government funding.

This is not to say that Women's Committees were not successful. In most local authorities they were, and some continue to be, successful in changing the local government agenda: persuading service-deliverers to consider the impact of their policies and practice on women. Labour local authorities, in response to feminists inside and outside the local authorities, have developed publicly funded child-care, and attempted to improve their street-lighting. It is now commonplace for local authorities to have equal opportunity personnel policies. The loss of Women's Committees means that many of the innovative changes in local government introduced in the 1980s will not be developed during the 1990s.

The most worrying aspect of the lament that the feminist movement no longer exists is its tendency to incorporate feminism into identity politics. This is best exemplified by a glance at the *Guardian* Women's Page. In the 1970s, the *Guardian* Women's Page published combative writers who would regularly reflect feminist debates, challenging many established ideas. Nowadays the Women's Page is barely distinguishable from other 'life-style' pages in the *Guardian* tabloid section. It concentrates on interviews with famous women. As I was writing this pamphlet, the Women's Page was filled with an interview with Benazir Bhutto, Prime Minister of Pakistan, holding her up as a feminist icon, and failing to mention the reality of many women's lives in Pakistan: widespread illiteracy, two-thirds of girls between 5 and 15 kept out of school, 15 million child labourers, 50% of the population without access to clean drinking water and 80% without proper sanitation (leading to 250,000 children under 5 dying in 1995 from diarrhoea), not to mention the relatively high incidence of rape, domestic violence and forced prostitution. Despite this, Bhutto's government spends 27% of its budget on defence, and just 1% on education. The International Monetary Fund approves, which only goes to show that the feminist agenda these days must directly challenge the ruling global economic orthodoxy if it is to rise above identity politics.

The women's movement may be more fragmented and less visible than in the 1970s, but its guiding ideas are more widespread among women of all ages than they ever were before. The media has decided that we do not exist, but that does not make it so. Women in Britain and around the world are organising at the grass-roots around issues both local and universal. Confronted by discrimination or harassment, they are more likely than ever to fight for redress. There is a movement, unfashionable, often misrepresented, sometimes derided but usually just ignored; and it is a movement that applies pressure for equality — at work, in the streets and at home — every day.

Think-tanks

Left-of-centre think-tanks like the Institute for Public Policy Research and Demos have been prominent in arguing that feminism either no longer exists or is no longer relevant.

The Institute for Public Policy Research was established in 1988 as a counterpart to the Tory Policy Studies Institute. Its board is chaired by Tessa Blackstone, and Charles Clarke (former adviser to Neil Kinnock), John Edmonds (General Secretary GMB), Patricia Hewitt and David Marquand (adviser to Tony Blair) are among its trustees. The IPPR has published a series of pamphlets on the family. It is interesting to trace the development of post-feminist ideas through these pamphlets. In 1990, *The Family Way* by Coote, Harman & Hewitt[27] argued that different forms of families need to be recognised by policy-makers, and that any family policy has to centre on the needs of children, and in particular to alleviate poverty amongst children. In 1993, Hewitt & Leach published *Social Justice, Children & Families*[28] as a contribution to the Commission on Social Justice. This again focused on poverty and children and looked at different mechanisms to distribute child benefit. Both these pamphlets, although ideologically part of the Labour Party's shift away from increases in public spending to forms of private social insurance, approached their subjects from an overtly feminist view. Hewitt and Leach condemned 'government ministers [who] have singled out lone parents — and particularly, unmarried teenage mothers — for their attack on the breakdown of the "family". Lone parents, it seems, are to blame for everything from the state of the public finances, to the inexorably rising crime rate. Benefit cuts, the withdrawal of public housing, new responsibilities for grandparents to maintain their grandchildren, even a lowering of the age of consent are all being canvassed by the Government in what is rapidly becoming a full-scale moral panic.' Hewitt and Leach took a non-judgemental view on different forms of family organisation, and concentrated on the need to use child benefit to alleviate child poverty.

In 1996, *Men & their children*[29] by Burgess & Ruxton was published with a fanfare of publicity. This pamphlet concentrated on the need for men to be involved in rearing their children. It makes a number of sensible points about involving men in child-birth and nurturing as well as the need for men to retain contact with their children if relationships break up. Within a feminist agenda, this would all be very well. But the pamphlet reads as though it were written from a premise that men, in particular, and more than women, do badly out of the present society. Above all, it is extraordinary that a pamphlet seeking to focus on the role of men in families should fail to mention domestic violence or child abuse, acts of violence, overwhelmingly perpetrated by men, which are profoundly destructive to families.

This is not to say that all men are violent and should have no contact with their children. But any policy seeking to look at men's involvement with their children must recognise that domestic violence and child abuse are serious problems, and require attention. In general, the pamphlet reads as though there are no differences in power between men and women, or that if there are, it is men who have less power than women. The emphasis of the IPPR seems to have moved away from alleviating child poverty to remedying alleged discrimination against men.

Another theme of IPPR's pamphlets has been the change in employment patterns and practices. In *About time — the revolution in work and family life*,[30] Patricia Hewitt postulates flexible working hours and casual labour as a benefit for women with families. She does not mention strong arm tactics from employers for women to work the hours that suit employers, nor the economic pressures on women to work long hours. The absence of any discussion on the effect of low pay on women is shocking. There is no mention of a minimum wage — a measure which overnight would improve the standards of living of millions of women — nor is there any critical analysis of the overall reduction in the number of full-time jobs available, and their replacement by part-time jobs.

Demos describes itself as 'an independent think-tank committed to radical solutions to long-term problems'. Its work has concentrated on attitudes rather than political activity. *No Turning Back: generations and the genderquake*,[31] by Helen Wilkinson, published in 1994, supposedly provided the statistical data for the argument that feminism is out-of-date.

Wilkinson argues that the old certainties in work and family life are disappearing, and that one reaction is despair, social and moral breakdown and scapegoating of different sections of society. Using a 1994 survey by Synergy Brand Values Ltd, which surveyed 2,500 people aged between 15 and 75, Wilkinson examines the lives of young women and men aged between 18 and 34. She finds that women's participation in economic activity has risen from 53%

in 1973 to 65% in 1991, and that the gender gap in earnings has narrowed from women earning 63% of male earnings in 1972 to 79% in 1991. Women's share of the household income has also risen, except in families receiving welfare benefits or on low pay. Women's self-employment is growing, more women are entering the professions and there has been a shift in employment from manufacturing industry to service jobs, thus benefiting women's employment prospects. Wilkinson notes that girls are outperforming boys at GCSE, A levels and at university, especially in science.

Nonetheless, she concedes that women make up only 3.72% of the membership of boards of major companies, and only 2.8% of senior managers and 9.8% of managers. Even women managers earn on average 16% less than their male counterparts. And the price of success is high — women managers are still less likely to be married and more likely to be childless than the average woman. Only 9% of employers provide help with child-care. 75% of all women continue to shoulder the main burdens of domestic labour, 67% of women in dual earner families. Women work an extra fifteen hours unpaid per week, compared to men. Part-time employment rose from 4 million to 5 million during the 1980s. Wilkinson welcomes this trend and sees flexible working conditions as advantageous for women. Of course, integration into the workforce is essential for women's liberation — but integration on whose terms? Wilkinson's own research indicates that this integration has not been on the basis of full equality with men. More significantly, she fails to deal with the reality that the 'flexibility' involved here is not for the convenience of the worker, female or male, but to enable the employer to maximise profit. The downside of flexibility is increased insecurity and exploitation; women who have been drawn into the workforce over the last twenty years, mainly in part-time, casual employment, find themselves in a position of extreme powerlessness in relation to their employers.

Wilkinson argues that women and girls have become more confident, less emotional, and more risk-taking than in the past. We are more interested in sexuality, and half of us have cohabited by the time we are 25. She cites business women using male escorts and nights out to see the Chippendales as a sign of our empowerment. Yet her own statistics indicate that the struggle for equality is far from complete. Only 13% of women think that having children is necessary in order to feel fulfilled; other women emphasised education, hobbies and an equal sharing of the domestic work. 79% of young women want to develop a career, 50% say having children is a goal (but not the sole goal). 43% of women would like help with child-care from their employers. 69% said that men should do the same domestic work as women. Although young women did not describe themselves as feminist, criticising the women's movement as being too strident and anti-male, their aspirations clearly reflected a feminist viewpoint. And the gap between those aspirations and reality of work, child-care and domestic labour is startling.

Nonetheless, Wilkinson concludes that feminism is out-of-date. She locates changes in the economy as the driving force of women's emancipation at work, and argues that the feminist agenda of rights is now superseded by a more complex set of issues, including discrimination against men and sexual harassment of men.

Like Wolf and Paglia, her assessment of feminism is defined by the progress made by middle-class, educated, professional women. Her paean to flexible working conditions entirely ignores the stark reality of low pay and poverty which defines the lives of an ever-increasing number of women, both in Britain and abroad. Her own statistics confirm that women have not achieved equality: whether in the world of the highly-paid manager or that of the lower-paid working-class woman. Far from supporting her proposal that women need to abandon the goal of equality for the one of 'diversity', as she suggests, Wilkinson's facts and figures confirm that the feminist movement's original goals must remain at the heart of any effort to make the mass of women's lives more fulfilling. Her survey does confirm that the feminist movement has achieved one very important objective: changing the attitudes and expectations certainly of young women if not of young men.

Labour Party

The women's organisation in the Labour Party has reflected the ups and downs of the broader women's movement. In the late 70s-early 80s, and coinciding with the rise of the left in the Labour Party, women activists, profoundly influenced by the second wave of feminism, began organising in ever greater numbers and to ever more radical purpose. They argued for an autonomous women's organisation, with women's representatives on the NEC being elected by the National Women's Conference, rather than the full Labour Party Conference, and with the right to place motions directly on the agenda of the Party Conference. They argued for policies such as a Ministry for Women. They succeeded in obtaining a commitment at Labour Party Conference that attacks on abortion rights should be opposed by the Labour Party in Parliament, rather than leaving Labour MPs to a free vote. For more than a decade, the Women's Conference was consistently one of the most left-wing voices in the Party.

Despite a sustained and well-argued campaign, the specific demands of the Women's Organisation were never achieved. The NEC Women's Section is still elected by the full Labour Party Conference and is not accountable to the Women's Conference or indeed to women at any level of the Party. In common with the rest of the Party, women's sections have declined in active membership. Women's Conference is now little more than a talking-shop, and increasingly not even that. Nowadays, it is used mainly as an opportunity for front benchers to make set-piece speeches.

Nonetheless, the Women's Organisation and its demands for more women representatives has had a profound impact on the

Party. In 1993, Labour Party Conference passed a commitment to all-women shortlists in half of all Tory-held marginals and Labour seats where the sitting MP was retiring. The proposal was controversial in the eyes of many Labour Party members. To many feminists active in the Women's Organisation, it was seen as an attempt to co-opt women activists and prevent them from persisting with the old demands for autonomy and power within the Party. Whilst we welcomed the commitment to increase the number of women MPs, we did not see this as a substitute for the general empowerment of women in the Party.

In addition, the mechanism of all-women shortlists was itself questioned. All-women shortlists in only half of Labour's marginals would not achieve equal numbers of women and men MPs until well into the 21st century. Since most all-women shortlists were in marginal seats that would probably change hands in each general election, the change in the safe seats would be even slower. And there was concern about the process of selecting which seats would have all-women shortlists. Marginals were asked to volunteer (one Constituency Labour Party which did volunteer was Leeds North East), but if there were insufficient volunteers, the Regional or National Party officials would have to select which seats would have to choose from an all-women shortlist. Some Constituency Parties feared that officials would use that power to block the candidacies of male dissidents who had a good chance of being selected. The experience of Slough Labour Party confirmed those fears.

The proposal was also attacked by opponents of positive discrimination. There were claims that positive discrimination measures were patronising, unfair to men and would not assist the feminist cause because 'second-rate women' would be selected who would not have been successful in a mixed shortlist. Feminists retorted that the Party had tried a number of different ways of increasing the representation of women in Parliament, including a requirement that every Parliamentary shortlist should have at least one woman on it, if a woman was nominated. None had made any discernible impact on the number of women being selected. In the end, two disgruntled male Party members, who had entertained hopes of being selected as prospective Parliamentary candidates, took the Labour Party to an industrial tribunal. It ruled in January 1996 that selecting a prospective Parliamentary candidate was akin to choosing an employee for an advertised job, and that therefore any attempts at positive discrimination were contrary to the Sex Discrimination Act. Rejecting its own legal advice, the National Labour Party decided not to appeal the decision and therefore all-women shortlists are no longer in use. In any case, feminists in the Party had suspected that all-women shortlists were falling out of fashion when, in July 1995, Blair had announced that because the measures had been sufficiently successful, ensuring that 25% of the Parliamentary Labour Party after the next general election would be women, they were no longer needed. Somehow, the Leader implied, advancement towards 50% representation would happen of its own accord; precisely how and when it would happen remained unspecified.

Over the years, the demands for an autonomous and powerful Women's Organisation and for increased representation of women's issues in Parliament had fallen down the political agenda, to be replaced by a concern simply to increase the number of women MPs in itself. As the Women's Organisation declined and some feminist activists left the Party out of frustration at its right-wing drift and refusal to take women's demands seriously, a number of 'women's networks' sprang up dedicated to helping individual women enter Parliament. Newsletters for the Labour Women's Network contained advice on writing CVs, addressing selection meetings and combining Parliamentary ambitions with a career and a family. Barbara Follett achieved fame by advising MPs how to dress. The tailored suit, preferably in Labour Party red, became *de rigeur* for women prospective Parliamentary candidates, giving rise to jokes about 'the shoulder-pad brigade'.

Emily's List, set up by Follett in 1992, offered cash to enable selected women candidates to attend meetings and canvass for support from party members. The process whereby a few women were chosen to receive funds remained entirely secret and unaccountable to women in the Party. This was not about women's empowerment, either within the Labour Party or within Parliament, but about the advancement of a self-selecting elite. The good and the great hid behind the long-standing and legitimate demand for increased women's representation in Parliament — but there was no indication that the particular women whose careers were promoted were actually committed to doing something concrete for women once they entered the House of Commons.

Of course it is unacceptable that, in 1996, only 9% of Parliament is female. The absence of women MPs inevitably means the absence of women's needs and demands from the larger political agenda. But having more women MPs in itself will not necessarily improve the lives of working-class women. The way to ensure that feminist demands are raised in Parliament is by having more women MPs committed to a broad programme for the betterment of all working-class women and accountable to a vibrant and democratic Women's Organisation. Unfortunately, most of the women prospective Parliamentary candidates selected to fight the next general election are more interested in docility and loyalty to the Labour Party leadership than arguing the feminist corner.

The Women's Organisation's demand for a Minister for Women, at Cabinet level, became Labour Party policy in the late 1980s. Jo Richardson served as Shadow Minister for Women until her death in 1994. Between 1994 and 1996, the proposal appeared to have been watered down — the department would not have Cabinet status or a Ministry and would only be a small unit with a watching brief on the government. The Cabinet commitment was restored in the 1996 Strategy for Women, but in the absence

31

of resources or concrete policy commitments it appears little more than a token gesture.

Policies to assist women have been among the major casualties of the Blair assault on public spending commitments. In 1992, John Smith set up the Labour Party's Commission on Social Justice, whose 'findings' were heavily influenced by the IPPR. When it reported in 1994, after Tony Blair had become Leader of the Party, it proposed a change in Labour's view of the welfare state. Instead of being an instrument for the redistribution of wealth, the welfare state was depicted as little more than a social insurance policy.

When it came to women's needs, the Commission drew on the IPPR's submissions on flexibility at work. Arguing, rightly, that when the welfare state was envisaged by Beveridge, it was based on the assumption that most families were two-parent families, with one male bread-winner, the Commission used the change in women's roles since the 1940s to argue that flexible working conditions benefited the whole family:

> 'the new challenge is to take advantage of increasingly flexible forms of employment to give men as well as women far greater choice as to how they combine employment, family, education, community activities and leisure in different ways and at different stages in their lives. In other words, we need to make flexibility work for rather than against employees, especially those with family responsibilities.'

Again, the emphasis is on individual choice rather than collective empowerment. And again, there is an almost wilful naiveté (or perhaps sheer ignorance) about the nature of the modern workplace. There is no discussion about employees required to work anti-social hours, about short-term contracts, about piece work or about pay on a commission basis. The Commission proposed funding for lone parents to have help with child-care as part of a Job, Education and Training programme. Interestingly, of the six goals listed for this JET programme, the goal concerning child-care is the least detailed. The Commission went on to argue that traditional, male, full-time employment was an out-of-date concept, welcomed the rise in part-time jobs and argued that men had to be convinced to apply for jobs in traditional 'female' spheres.

It is a pity that it takes such a blunt instrument as mass unemployment to break down gender segregation in employment. It is also a pity that the Commission's attitude was to welcome the shift from full-time to part-time employment, rather than attempting to reinvigorate the economy to create more full-time jobs and genuine flexibility for workers. The Commission does recommend contract compliance in the public sector; this would allow local and central government to insist that private companies bidding for public sector contracts offer equal opportunities for women. This was a tool much used by Labour local authorities in the early 80s until prohibited by government legislation. It is widely accepted and practised by public authorities in the USA. Finally, the Commission recommends a comprehensive anti-discrimination law, prohibiting discrimination on the grounds of age, sexuality or disability, as well as the current sex, race and marital status. All most welcome, though largely disregarded by the Labour leadership. The Commission also argued that child benefit should remain a universal benefit, in contrast to the recent proposals to abolish child benefit for 16-18 year olds in full-time education.

The proposals of the Commission on Social Justice provided an interesting insight into the thinking of some of the ideologues behind the Labour Party leadership. They took from the IPPR a belief in individual achievement rather than collective action, and a commitment to regulation rather than social ownership. They also took a completely uncritical view of flexible working conditions, and a belief that the world of work had changed to such an extent that a return to full employment was not possible. Their proposals were attractive to middle-class professional families: help with child-care, allowing both partners to combine decently paid jobs with flexible hours, choices between full-time and part-time, employment protection and generous maternity and paternity leave. But they did not touch the lives of millions who are employed in part-time jobs because they cannot find full-time jobs, who are badly paid and therefore forced to take several part-time jobs just to make ends meet. Those women would love well-paid flexible working conditions, but their immediate concern is to earn enough to secure a decent life for themselves and their families. They are working to live, not living to work; their priorities are decent pay and employment protection.

In 1995, Peace At Home, Labour's policy on domestic violence, was launched by Cherie Booth, who enjoys no elected position within the Party (other than the ex-officio one of 'Leader's Wife'). The document reflected the innovative work on domestic violence undertaken by Labour local authorities. It was the first document on domestic violence ever issued by a major political party in Britain. However, it was notable that the funding commitments had changed considerably since the 1994 Strategy for Women, published barely 18 months earlier. There are commitments to review and improve domestic violence legislation, and to strengthen the law on rape and the disclosure of sexual history. Many of the specific commitments are devolved to local authorities: a Labour government will require local authorities to consider crime and crime prevention when making decisions about planning and services. It calls for a network of refuges, but it is unclear whether the money will be made available by central government to fund these refuges. Without funding, many of the changes proposed will be ineffective.

The document also fails to place actions against domestic violence in context with other Labour Party proposals. For example, making legal remedies for domestic violence simpler and easier to obtain will only benefit women with resources to pay lawyers, or women eligible for legal aid. Given that only 27% of the population is eligible for legal aid, a refusal to increase legal aid funding effectively prevents many women from seeking redress for domestic violence through the Courts. While the document relates domestic violence to homelessness and poor housing, and calls for a phased release of local authority housing capital receipts to allow local authorities to build more houses, it makes no mention of reversing the government's current proposals on homelessness, which will prevent local authorities providing permanent accommodation to women fleeing domestic violence. There is no definition of domestic violence, rape or sexual assault. And there is certainly no consideration of any broader proposals, such as improvements in public transport, which would be required to make any substantial improvement in women's safety.

In July 1996, an up-dated Strategy for Women was published by the Labour Party. It is anxious to distance itself from any negative perceptions of feminism — Tessa Jowell states in the introduction 'New Labour's policies are not about narrow sexual politics'. As in all Labour Party documents, it competently criticises government policies that affect women's lives, and compares those policies with the reality of working-class women's lives. However, as in all recent Labour Party documents, the solutions it offers are woefully inadequate.

The specific commitments are:
- access to parental leave;
- a national minimum wage (but no figure);
- simplification of the equal pay legislation;
- the New Deal for the Under 25s to get young people into work;
- partnership with employers to meet local child-care needs;
- homework clubs;
- new technology in schools;
- cutting class sizes to a minimum of 30 for 5, 6 and 7 year olds;
- a review of the law relating to rape and domestic violence;
- flexibility in the present benefits system;
- a 'flexible decade' in retirement;
- phased release of council housing capital receipts;

- ending the two-tier access to the NHS created by GP fundholding;
- easily accessible family planning and well-women clinics;
- reviewing the road-building programme;
- flexible services for carers;
- anti-discrimination measures for people with disabilities;
- increasing the numbers of women on management boards for the arts, sport and the media.

Other than the commitment to introduce a Minister for Women at Cabinet level, there is not one proposal in this document which cannot be found elsewhere in Labour's programme. Public spending commitments, other than those paid for by the windfall tax or the abolition of the assisted places scheme, are scrupulously avoided. Terms such as 'flexible services' are bandied around, but no money will be available to improve existing services. It is hard to see how services and support for carers, who are already massively over-stretched, can be made more flexible without some increase in spending on them.

The Labour Party is struggling to reconcile its attempts to seem more woman-friendly with its prohibition on increases in public spending. It is certainly welcome that the Party is addressing the issue of domestic violence, but all attempts will be mere window-dressing if there are no commitments to fund refuges or other services for women fleeing domestic violence.

It is not surprising to find the same Labour leadership which extols flexibility at work also poses as a champion of family values and opponent of single mothers. The contradiction is only apparent: both positions absolve the state and employers from larger social responsibilities for human welfare, and both place the burden of survival on the individual's moral fibre.

Feminist life outside Britain

The 1995 UN Women's Conference in Beijing was a recognition of the importance of women's politics and of feminism. The Conference was attended not only by government representatives but also by hundreds of Non-Governmental Organisations (NGOs), reflecting women's experiences from around the world. It dealt with the bread-and-butter issues that make a real difference to the reality of women's lives: reproductive rights, malnutrition, poverty, access to education and health, violence against women, the environment. Feminism has been derided as of interest only to privileged Western women. The vibrancy of the NGO side of Beijing showed that women's groups and voluntary organisations function throughout the world, including in societies dominated by fundamentalist and anti-women politics. International solidarity amongst women is vital in a world where women play an increasing role in the formal economy — but work longer hours for lower pay than men.[32]

Women's demands are now taken up in most progressive political movements throughout the world. In South Africa, for example, abortion on demand is now ANC policy, and the interim South African constitution contains a clause prohibiting discrimination on the basis of race, sex, creed or sexual orientation. In many countries, feminist activity is about survival at the grass-roots: feminists run health clinics, child-care centres, literacy programmes in areas where the state fails to provide them. And there is hardly a society on earth where there are not campaigns of some kind for women's reproductive rights and against violence against women.

Increasingly in the future, women in the first world will learn from women in the Third World as both come under the hammer of IMF prescriptions. And as women lead struggles for collective provision, and for respect for themselves and their environment, capitalism may well find that the integration of women into the workforce has created a new global army of resistance.

I have confidence that feminism, as an active political movement and a developing ideology, can and will survive. Whilst women's status has risen, the economic reality is that women are still paid less than men, there is still sexual segregation, insufficient child-care and violence against women is still a significant part of many women's lives. And much of what we have won in the past needs to be defended anew, not least our reproductive rights.

But the change in attitudes is deeply encouraging. All the surveys show that, despite young women's reluctance to identify themselves as feminist, they believe that they have the right to develop their careers and to be treated equally, without regard for their appearance, and live their lives in safety.

Women's political activity continues. The Pall Mall Hillingdon Hospital strikers are a group of 54 Asian women who have been picketing the hospital day in and day out for months in support of their claim against wage cuts. One of my most rewarding experiences has been campaigning with a group of working-class women who successfully occupied a local authority nursery to save it from closure three years' ago.

The Body Shop now has a women's policy officer. As I heard her address a conference of local government women's officers and Councillors, and neatly talk herself through the difficulties of a feminist promoting the cosmetics industry, I was struck by the irony of feminism becoming part of the big business agenda. Here was proof both that feminism had penetrated the mainstream and that it needed to be extricated for identity politics if it was to serve the needs of the majority of women.

In the teeth of fierce resistance, feminism has achieved a widespread acceptance of the value of equal treatment. That value conflicts sharply with the reality of many women's lives today, and the resulting gap between expectations and reality inevitably sparks campaigns for social change. Despite the concerted attempt to persuade us all that we live in a post-feminist world, I am confident that the basic demands and perspectives of feminism are as valid today as they were twenty-five or thirty years ago, and that women will not cease to organise as women until they have achieved equality.

References

1. Rowbotham, Segal & Wainwright, *Beyond the Fragments: Feminism and the Making of Socialism*, Merlin Press, 1979.

2. Faludi, *Backlash: The Undeclared War Against Women*, Chatto & Windus, 1992.

3. For a discussion on feminism, post-modernism and post-feminism, along with a very useful overview of the development of the Second Wave feminist movement, see Wheelehan, *Modern Feminist Thought: From the Second Wave to 'Post-Feminism'* Edinburgh University Press, 1995.

4. Figes, *Because of her sex: The Myth of Equality for Women in Britain*, Macmillan, 1994.

5. Mooney *The Hidden Figure: Domestic Violence in North London*, Islington Council, 1993.

6. Wilkinson, *No Turning Back: generations and the genderquake* Demos, 1994, quoting 1991 figures. There are a variety of figures quoted in different books, all are between 70-80% and the 79% figure, taken from the New Earnings Survey, seems to be the most widely quoted.

7. Wilkinson, *No Turning Back: generations and the genderquake*, Demos, 1994.

8. Figes, *Because of her sex: The Myth of Equality for Women in Britain*, Macmillan, 1994.

9. Department for Education and Employment March 1993 figures.

10. Wilkinson, *No Turning Back: generations and the genderquake*, Demos, 1994.

11. Joshi 'The Cost of Caring' in Glendinning & Millar (eds) *Women & Poverty in Britain, the 1990s*, Harvester Wheatsheaf, 1992.

12. Lonsdale 'Patterns of Paid Work' in Glendinning & Millar (eds) *Women & Poverty in Britain, the 1990s*, Harvester Wheatsheaf, 1992.

13. Land 'Whatever happened to the social wage?' in Glendinning & Millar (eds) *Women & Poverty in Britain, the 1990s*, Harvester Wheatsheaf, 1992.

14. Two-thirds of men prosecuted for rape involved men who were known to the woman. 44% of women who are killed are killed by their husband or former lover. 8 out of 10 know their killer — see Radford & Stanko, 'Violence against women and children' in Hester, Kelly & Radford (eds) *Women, Violence and Male Power*, Oxford University Press, 1996.

15. Lees & Gregory, *Rape and Sexual Assault: A Study of Attrition*, 1993, Islington Council.

16. *Guardian* 1 July 1996.

17. Wolf, *The Beauty Myth*, Chatto & Windus, 1990.

18. Wolf, *Fire with Fire: the new female power and how it will change the 21st century*, Chatto & Windus, 1993.

19. Paglia, *Sexual Personae: Art and Decadence from Nefertiti to Emily Dickinson*,

Harmondsworth: Penguin Books, 1992 and *Vamps & Tramps*, Viking 1995 among other publications.

20. *Vamps & Tramps* ibid.
21. Mooney, ibid.
22. *Vamps & Tramps* ibid.
23. quoted in Whelehan, ibid.
24. literature on child abuse is reviewed in Hester, Kelly & Radford, *Women, Violence & Male Power* ibid.
25. quoted in genderquake, Demos, Wilkinson.
26. quoted in Everywoman, Sept 95.
27. IPPR, 1990.
28. IPPR, 1993.
29. IPPR, 1996.
30. IPPR, 1993.
31. Demos, 1994.
32. *More and Better Jobs for Women — An Action Guide*, Lin Leam Lim, International Labour Organisation, July 1996.

Printed by the Russell Press Ltd. Tel: (0115) 9784505.

Published in October 1996 by Spokesman for European Labour Forum, Bertrand Russell House, Gamble Street, Nottingham, NG7 4ET. Tel: (0115) 9708318. Fax: (0115) 9420433.

Publications list/subscription details available on request.